I0114387

How We Became US

A Memory Book for Families with Multiple Aliens, Plushies, or Traveling Toys

Created by Bayyo and Doccy
and You!

ne World of US!

All of Us

How We Became US

Names & Adoption Dates

Where We Live

What Makes Us Us

US at Home

US Having Adventures

US at work

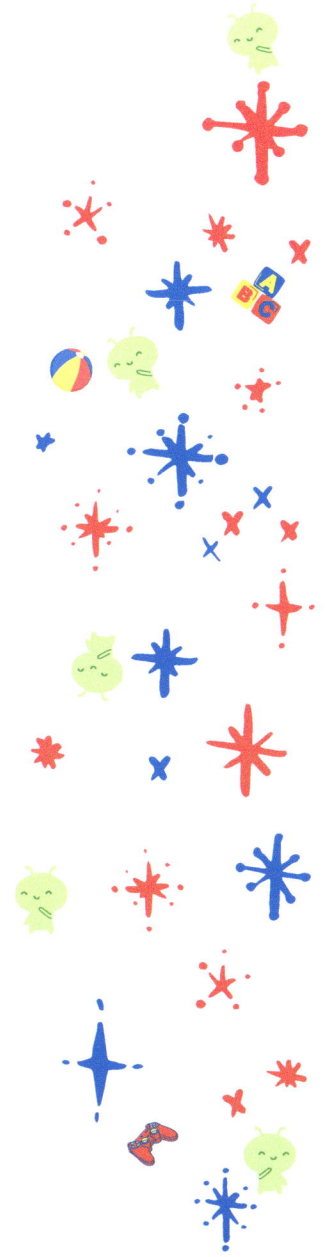

US at Play

US Being casual

US Being Fancy

US on vacation

US at Holiday Time

US Celebrating

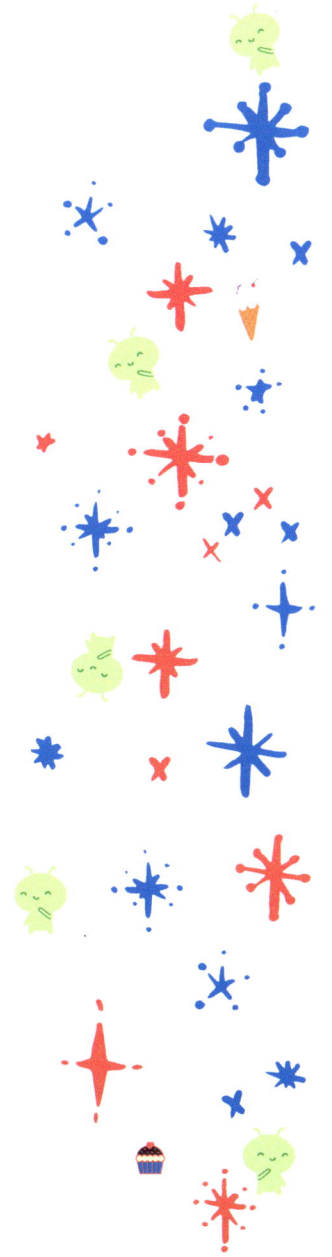

US Making Missy Jif (mischief)

US Doing Hobbies

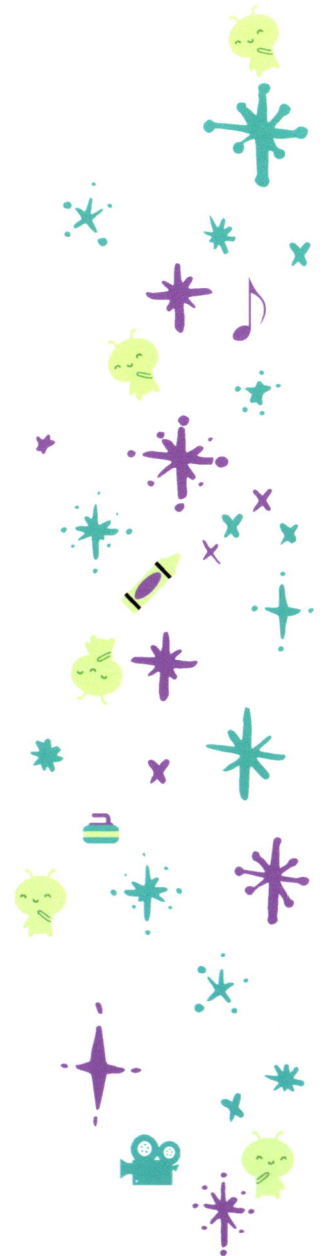

US at Snacktime

US at Bedtime

US Being Cutey Cute

That iS ALL THE TIME

What We Love About US

We Will Always Remember

ThiS iS US

We are Amazing

ThiS iS LOVe

Dedicated With Love
to All Our Fwens

💚

Across the Galaxy
and Beyond

Ideas for How To Use this Book

Open spaces are for you! Each page is like a stage for you to create your story! You can leave the book as it is and create your story aloud, by talking, or in your imagination all by yours

Or You Might Try...

Handwriting * Cutting and Pasting Typed Text * Photographs

Drawings * collage * Stickers *

Decorative tape * Postcards * Letters * Stamps * Mementos

Personal Memories * Quotes * Lists * Poems *

And More!

Not Sure if a particular ink or adhesive will work on these pag

Maybe test it in a small area of one of the back pages and give time to dry to see.

Have fun!

Created by

BayYo and Doccy

+

You!

Text and Layout Copyright © BayYo and Doccy
BayYo and Doccy LLC

First Hardcover Edition 2022
ISBN 978 - 1 - 7375420 - 6 - 3

ights Reserved. No part of this book may be copied or transmitted in any form or
ner including, but not limited to, photography, scanning, photocopying, audio recording,
leo recording, or digital recording, without written permission from the publishers.

ted sharing on social media permitted, provided that no reproducible (high def, close-
images appear and quotations are short and appear with full credit to the authors.

More Books from Bayyo and Doccy

Our Galactic Community
A keepsake Book of Fwendship and Love
ISBN: 978 – 1 – 7375420 – 0 – 1

First Year on Earth
A keepsake Book of Our Little Alien
(A Baby Book for Your Adopted Intergalactic Child)
ISBN: 978 – 7375420 – 1 – 8

Our Unusual Families
A Tale of One Little Alien's Unusual Families
and A Celebration of Unusual Families Everywhere
ISBN: 978 – 1 – 7375420 – 4 – 9

Learn More about Bayyo and Doccy
Insta: @Dr.T_Writes
BayyoandDoccy.com

Learn More about Our Books
OurGalacticMemories.com

Help Support Our Creative Projects and Cheer
Ko-Fi.com/BayyoandDoccy

Contact Us
Email: BayyoMail@gmail.com
Fwenmail: PO Box 55, Palm Beach, FL 33480 USA

Enjoy the Book, Fwens!

www.ingramcontent.com/pod-product-compliance
Lightning Source LLC
Chambersburg PA
CBHW040805300326

41914CB00064B/1609